NO LONGER PROPERTY OF
SEATTLE PUBLIC LIBRARY

D0461617

JUN 03 2017

REWARD

To Great-Uncle Sam, Pinkerton Detective!
-MM

To Ava
-AC

Text copyright © 2017 Marissa Moss
Illustrations copyright © 2017 April Chu
Book design by Simon Stahl

All rights reserved. No part of this book may be reproduced in any form or by any electronic or mechanical means including information storage and retrieval systems - except in case of brief quotations embodied in critical articles or reviews - without permission in writing from its publisher, Creston Books, LLC.

CIP data for this book is available from the Library of Congress.

Published by Creston Books, LLC

www.crestonbooks.co

Illustrations created with pencil on paper, then colored digitally.
Type set in Garamond, Century, Outstanding, and Archive Antiqua.
Source of Production: Worzalla Books, Stevens Point, Wisconsin
Printed and bound in the United States of America
1 2 3 4 5

FSC
www.fsc.org

MIX
Paper from responsible sources
FSC® C002589

KATE WARNE

PINKERTON DETECTIVE

Kate Warne: Pinkerton Detective

By
Marissa Moss

Illustrated by
April Chu

Creston Books

Kate read the newspaper advertisement for the third time:

WANTED: DETECTIVE

MUST BE OBSERVANT, DETERMINED, FEARLESS, AND WILLING TO TRAVEL. PINKERTON AGENCY 353 MICHIGAN AVE, CHICAGO

She had no experience at all, but the job called to her. It would be so much more interesting than taking in laundry or teaching school. First, she'd have to figure out how to present herself. Nobody would hire a single woman, not in 1856. Better to say she was a widow.

Kate had never known her mother. She'd been raised by her father, a printer, in a house full of books. Now that her father was also dead, Kate was on her own. Somehow she had to find a way to support herself.

She turned to the things that had filled her childhood, the characters who had kept her company as she grew up – books. Her life could be a story, just like one of her favorites. She could be whoever she wanted to be, so long as she told the tale well. And she knew just what story to tell.

So Kate Carter became Kate Warne. She put on her best dress and walked the three miles to the Pinkerton Agency, careful to keep the hem of her skirt free of dust. Nerves fluttered up her throat as she opened the door. She left Kate Carter behind as she walked in. Now she was Kate Warne, exactly the kind of person you'd want to hire as a detective.

Allan Pinkerton thought she was a client. So he took out his notebook and started writing down his observations, the first thing any good detective does with a new case.

"She was above the medium height, slender, graceful in her movements, and perfectly self-possessed in her manner." He noted her "brown hair, pale, broad face, dark blue eyes," and that her expression was "sharp, decisive, filled with fire." Right away, he knew he'd take on her case, whatever it was.

Only she said she wasn't a client at all. She was applying for a job.

Pinkerton told her he had no need for a washerwoman or cook.

"That's fortunate," Kate said, keeping her voice firm. "Since I'm not interested in those positions." She opened up her bag and pulled out the help wanted ad.

Pinkerton frowned. "Being a detective is physically demanding, dangerous work. Not at all the sort of thing a woman could do."

"I think it's precisely the sort of thing a woman should do," Kate answered. "As a woman, I can go places your male agents can't. A criminal may confide in his wife or lady friend. And those women will talk to another woman. Not to a man."

She was so certain, so self-assured, Pinkerton hesitated. "Let me think it over. Come back tomorrow and you'll have your answer."

The next day, Kate came as soon as the office opened. The way she held herself convinced Pinkerton. "Today you've made some history. You're now the first woman detective in the country."

Pinkerton handed her a folder:

The Adams Express Case

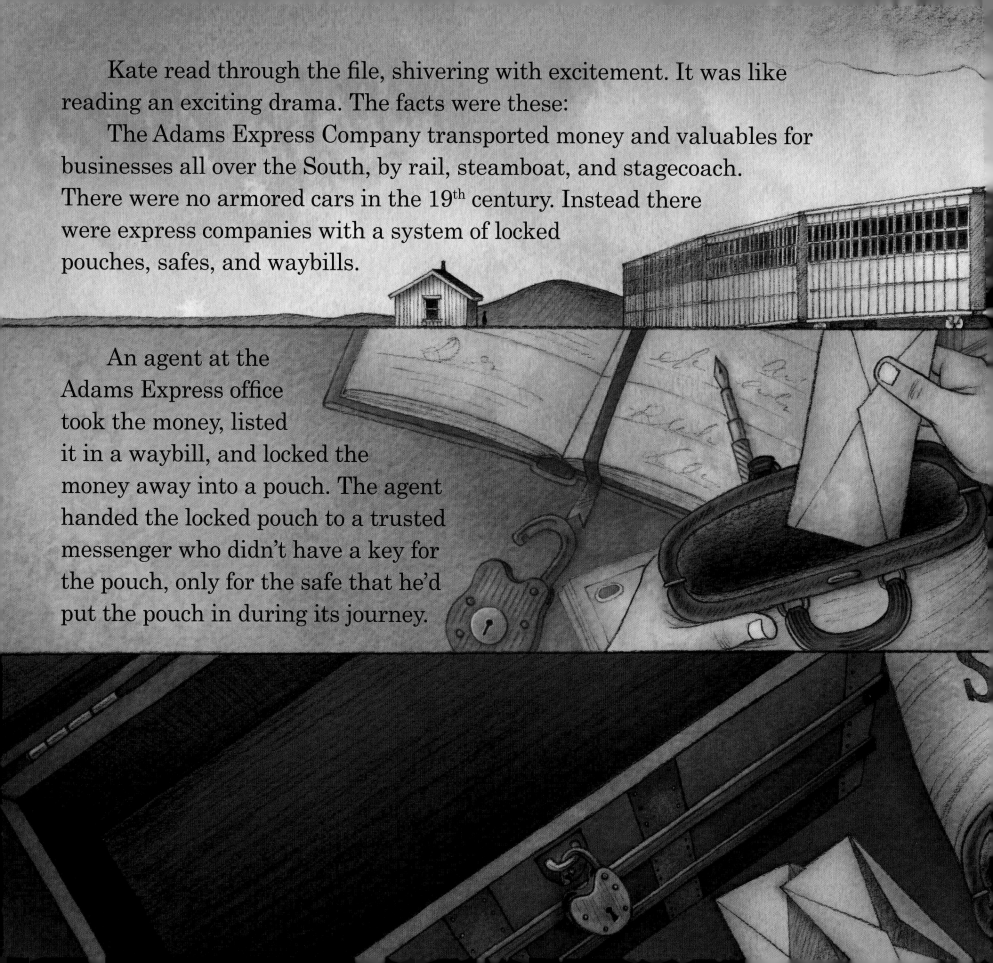

Kate read through the file, shivering with excitement. It was like reading an exciting drama. The facts were these:

The Adams Express Company transported money and valuables for businesses all over the South, by rail, steamboat, and stagecoach. There were no armored cars in the 19th century. Instead there were express companies with a system of locked pouches, safes, and waybills.

An agent at the Adams Express office took the money, listed it in a waybill, and locked the money away into a pouch. The agent handed the locked pouch to a trusted messenger who didn't have a key for the pouch, only for the safe that he'd put the pouch in during its journey.

So the pouch was doubly protected: by the lock on it and the lock around it on the safe. Each lock was specially constructed to be impossible to pick or cut open.

Once the messenger arrived at the destination, he unlocked the safe and handed the still-locked pouch to another agent at the arrival office.

So when $40,000 disappeared from four different packages, all in the same pouch, the company suspected one of their own workers. Who else had the keys? Who else could get at the pouch?

The main suspect: Nathan Maroney, the manager of the Montgomery office, where the packages had originated. The four packages with their large amounts of cash were written up on the waybills, then locked inside the pouch, which Maroney sealed up in the Montgomery office safe. The next morning, Maroney handed the pouch to the messenger, Mr. Chase, who delivered it to Atlanta. There the pouch was unlocked and found to be empty. Where had the money gone? And how?

Could Mr. Chase also be a suspect?

Kate thought so, but then she read the statement from Mr. Hall.

Mr. Hall, the Atlanta agent, brought the pouch back to Montgomery and confronted Maroney with it. "What happened?" he demanded. "Where's the money?"

Maroney looked at the pouch carefully, facing the window for better light. He turned back to Mr. Hall triumphantly.

"See, there! It's been cut!"

Sure enough, there were two cuts in an L-shape, large enough to wiggle fingers inside and draw out the money.

"Chase must have done it," Maroney insisted.

But Hall had examined the pouch himself. It hadn't been cut before.

THE ARREST:

Maroney was taken to jail on suspicion of embezzlement. But the only evidence was the freshly-slit pouch, according to a single witness, Mr. Hall. That wasn't enough to convict Maroney.

Kate leaned back, thinking. She imagined the scene in her head, counting the money, writing up the waybills, locking the pouches. She remembered hucksters performing the shell game, hiding a shell or a pea under one of three cards, and rapidly moving them while gamblers guessed which card hid the shell.

"It *was* Maroney and I know how he did it!"

"How?" Pinkerton asked.

"It's like one of those card tricks," Kate explained. "While Chase was writing up the waybill, Maroney showed him the notes, counted them, read out the amount, then slipped the bills in the package. Only really, he must have slipped the money *behind* the package, into an open desk drawer. Chase wouldn't be looking closely, he was busy writing down the numbers. And he trusted Maroney. So the money never went in the pouch! And Maroney had a drawer full of cash."

"Yes," Pinkerton agreed. "I thought the same. But a theory isn't proof. We need a confession. I'm sending another agent, John White, to jail with Maroney. He'll act the part of a thief clever enough to bribe his way out of prison. His job is to get Maroney to trust him. Yours is to approach Maroney's wife. She can lead you to the money – if you can get her to confide in you."

Kate was on the case! On the train to Pennsylvania, where Maroney's wife Belle was staying with her sister, Kate developed a plan. She would become "Madame Imbert," the sad wife of man who was in prison for forgery.

She moved into a hotel near Belle's house, so it was easy to run into her at meals and while walking in the nearby gardens. Kate was careful not to approach Belle, but to be the kind of person Belle would want to know. She felt like she was playing a part in one of her books.

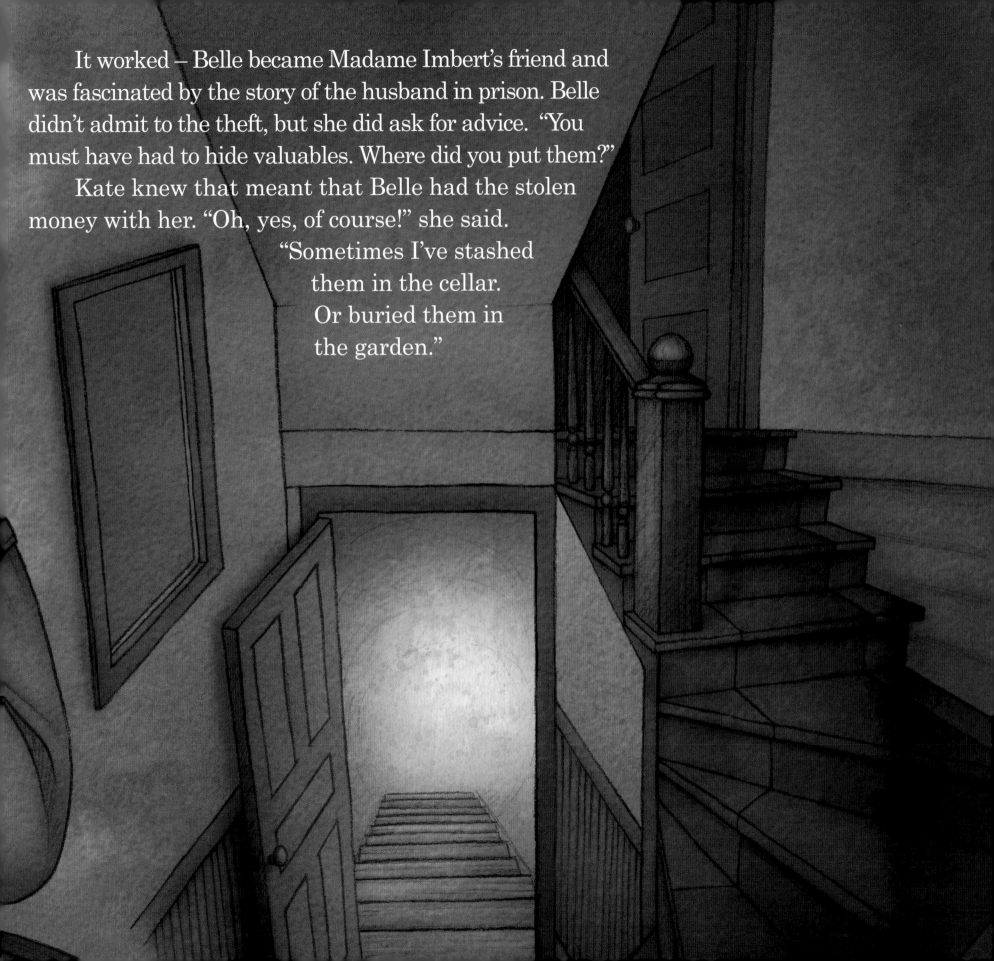

It worked – Belle became Madame Imbert's friend and was fascinated by the story of the husband in prison. Belle didn't admit to the theft, but she did ask for advice. "You must have had to hide valuables. Where did you put them?"

Kate knew that meant that Belle had the stolen money with her. "Oh, yes, of course!" she said. "Sometimes I've stashed them in the cellar. Or buried them in the garden."

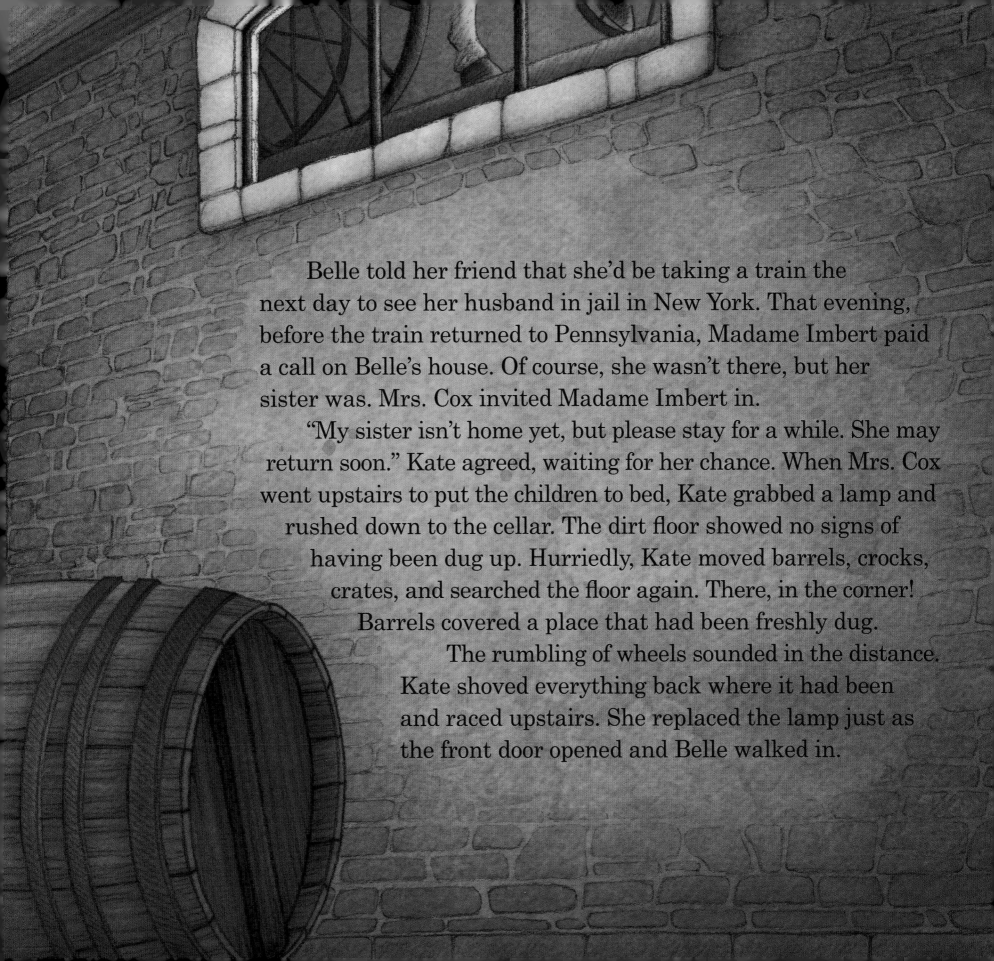

Belle told her friend that she'd be taking a train the next day to see her husband in jail in New York. That evening, before the train returned to Pennsylvania, Madame Imbert paid a call on Belle's house. Of course, she wasn't there, but her sister was. Mrs. Cox invited Madame Imbert in.

"My sister isn't home yet, but please stay for a while. She may return soon." Kate agreed, waiting for her chance. When Mrs. Cox went upstairs to put the children to bed, Kate grabbed a lamp and rushed down to the cellar. The dirt floor showed no signs of having been dug up. Hurriedly, Kate moved barrels, crocks, crates, and searched the floor again. There, in the corner! Barrels covered a place that had been freshly dug.

The rumbling of wheels sounded in the distance. Kate shoved everything back where it had been and raced upstairs. She replaced the lamp just as the front door opened and Belle walked in.

Belle was suspicious. "What's that on your dress?" She pointed at Kate's skirts, dirty from the cellar.

Kate brushed at her dress. "That must be from when I stumbled on my way here."

But she worried that she hadn't put everything back just so in the cellar and Belle would find out. She ran to Mr. Rivers, the Pinkerton agent assigned to follow Belle, and asked him to sneak in through the window.

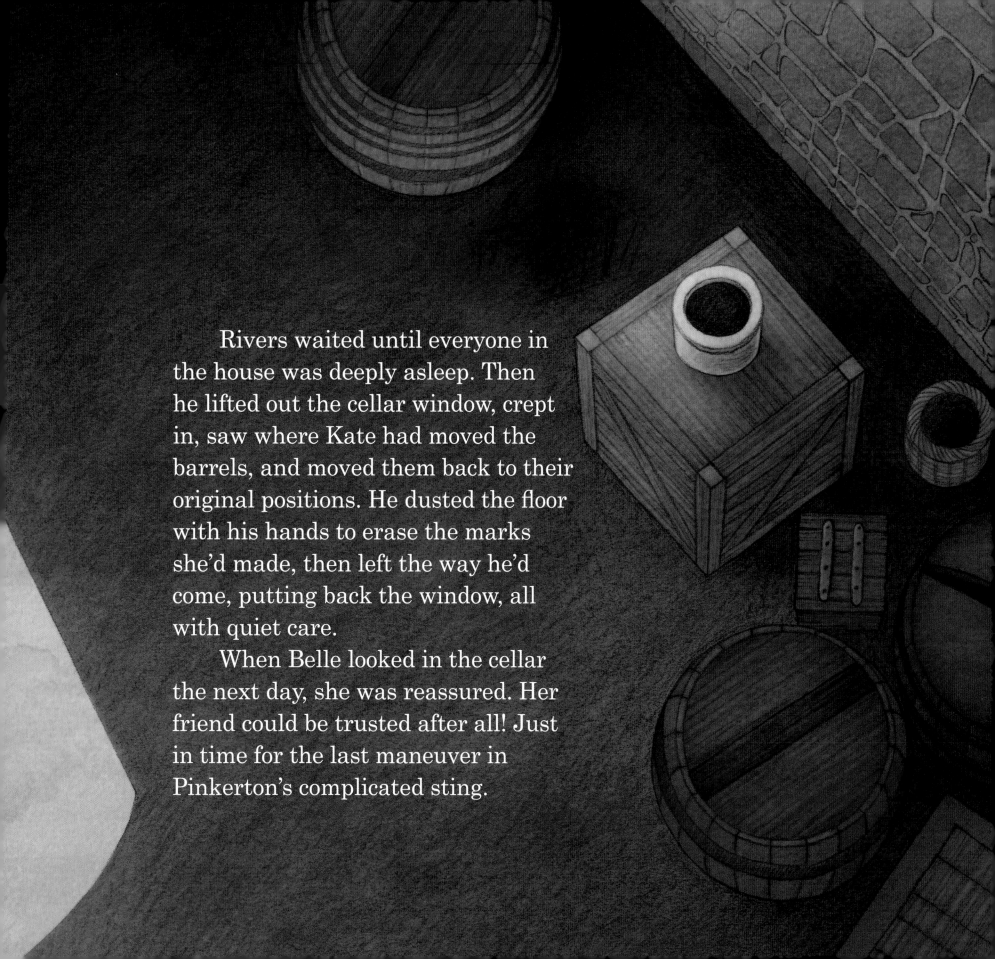

Rivers waited until everyone in the house was deeply asleep. Then he lifted out the cellar window, crept in, saw where Kate had moved the barrels, and moved them back to their original positions. He dusted the floor with his hands to erase the marks she'd made, then left the way he'd come, putting back the window, all with quiet care.

When Belle looked in the cellar the next day, she was reassured. Her friend could be trusted after all! Just in time for the last maneuver in Pinkerton's complicated sting.

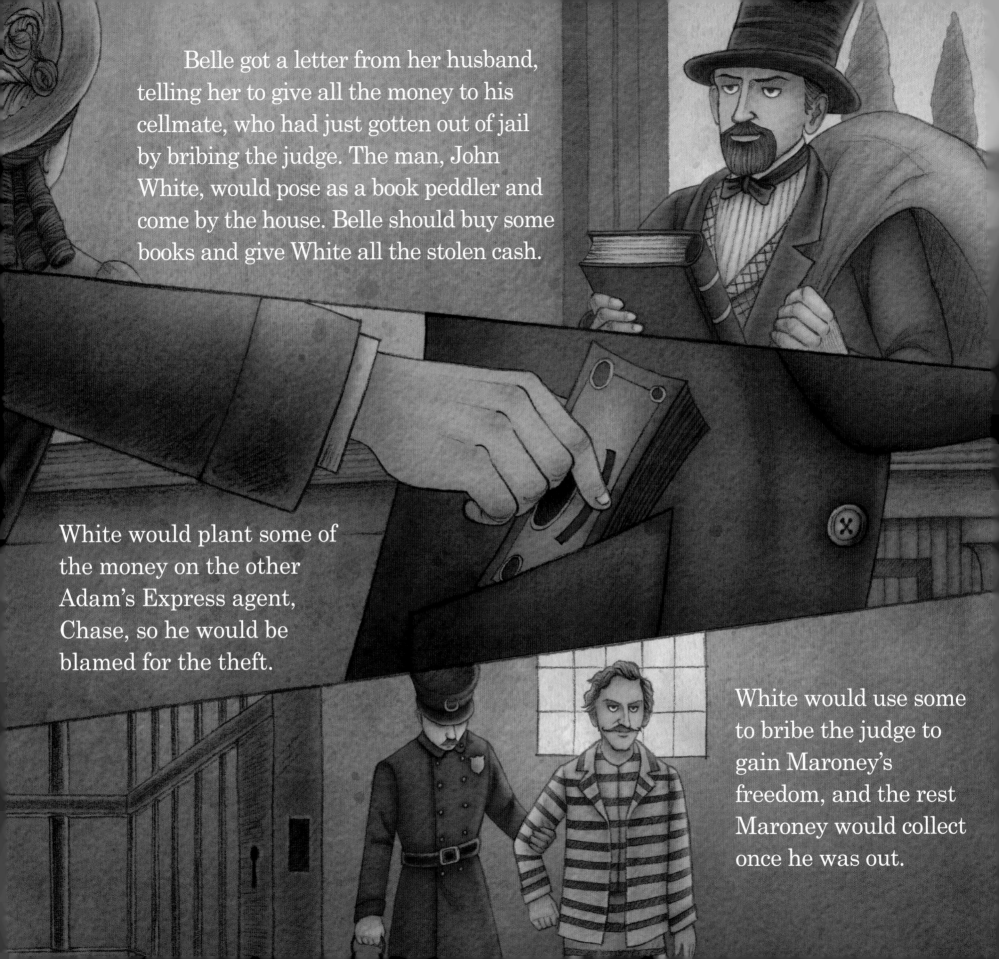

Belle got a letter from her husband, telling her to give all the money to his cellmate, who had just gotten out of jail by bribing the judge. The man, John White, would pose as a book peddler and come by the house. Belle should buy some books and give White all the stolen cash.

White would plant some of the money on the other Adam's Express agent, Chase, so he would be blamed for the theft.

White would use some to bribe the judge to gain Maroney's freedom, and the rest Maroney would collect once he was out.

Belle didn't trust this John White at all. She showed the letter to her good friend, Madame Imbert.

"What should I do?" she wailed. "How can I trust all that money, everything we have, to this stranger?"

Kate knew that John White was also a Pinkerton agent. Her job now was to convince Belle to go along with the plan. That meant being careful not to offer too much advice. Not to be pushy. To hesitate at just the right times. She said just what Belle needed to hear.

"If I could help my husband out of prison, I'd do anything." She sighed. And that was enough.

When White
came to the house
the next day selling
his wares, Belle and
Madame Imbert
were waiting for him.

"Do you wish to buy any books?" He handed Belle a novel, which he opened to reveal a note. "This one should interest you." The note said:

My dearest wife: This is the book-peddler. You will want to buy books from him. Buy what you want. Give him the packages from me. He is honest. All is well.   *–Nat*

Belle stood frozen.

"Have you no message for the man?" Kate gently prodded. "Perhaps you could meet him later, down the lane."

"Yes, I'll meet you there at 2 pm," Belle directed. She turned back to the house.

"Hurry," urged Kate, no longer gentle. "You must do as your husband asked."

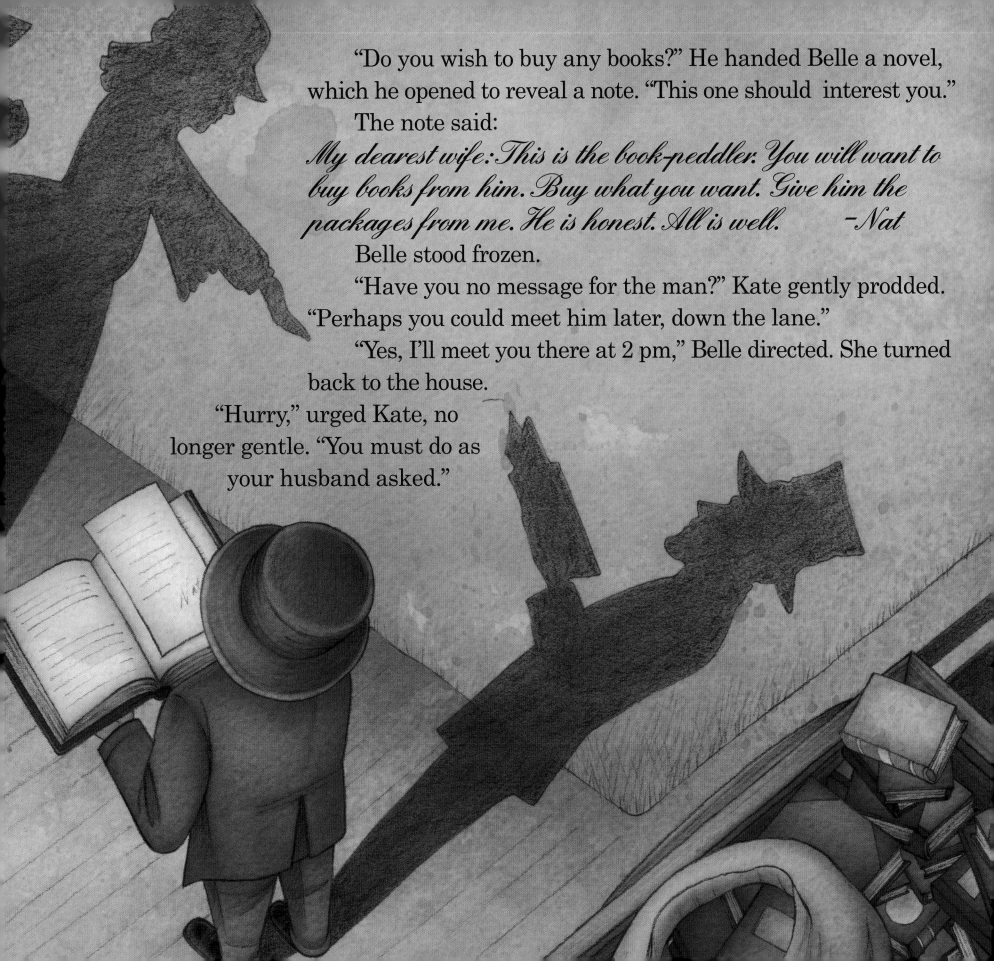

Belle called for her sister and brother-in-law. Together with her friend, they all went down to the cellar.

"Should we really do this?" asked Mr. Cox.

"You fools!" Kate was no longer mild. The money was so close! She grabbed the spade and prepared to dig herself. "This is your chance to free Mr. Maroney! You must do what's best for him."

"Alright, I'll do it!" Mr. Cox took the shovel and dug deep underground until he found a bulky package wrapped in oil skin. Kate snatched the bundles of cash, making sure to get all of it.

Then she and Belle took the horse and carriage down the lane, waiting for the bookseller. When they found him, Kate came forward first. "May we have some books?"

White offered a satchel full of novels. Kate grabbed it, dumped the books into the carriage, and shoved the cash, hidden in newspapers, into the satchel. Then the women drove off in one direction, the man in the other.

Kate felt jittery with excitement. She'd done it! And she'd used books to help crack the case, not just in coming up with her character, but in getting the money back! She'd traded stories for cash, books for justice.

Maroney, sure that the judge was safely bribed, went to trial with a smug smile on his face. But then the first witness was called, a Mr. John White. Hearing the name, Maroney paled. He whispered to his lawyer, abruptly changing his plea from not-guilty to guilty.

As for the original stolen $40,000, all of it was recovered in that satchel, except for $400. And the reputation of the Pinkerton agency was made. So was Kate Warne's.

WANTED!

WE NEVER SLEEP.

REWARD!

Back in Chicago, Pinkerton put her on all his toughest cases, but she also had a new responsibility.

So when Hattie Lawton came into the office, Kate knew she didn't want to be a secretary or a maid. "You must be here for the detective position," Kate said.

Hattie nodded. "Yes, I saw from the newspaper that you're hiring."

Kate smiled. "We have a women's division now and I'm in charge of it. So tell me your story, what makes you think you'd be a good Pinkerton agent?"

Kate hired Hattie. And more women after her. They were some of Pinkerton's strongest agents. But the best of all was Kate Warne. She played many different parts, acted in many different stories, and solved many different crimes. Her most important role was her first: Kate Warne, Pinkerton agent, the first woman detective in the country.

AUTHOR'S NOTE

Kate Warne's real name and history are a mystery. Was she a widow as she claimed, or a young woman re-inventing herself to make her own way? What we do know about her is that she was America's first woman detective – and highly successful. She was instrumental in solving the Adams Express Case, a high profile theft that established the reputation of the Pinkerton Agency as the best in the country. Before Pinkerton, detectives were looked upon as sleazy. As Judge John P. Vincent warned jurors when considering detectives' testimony, "The character of the detective – and it is simply another word for spy – has always been and always will be, an unpopular one. There is an element in human nature – and it is an element that humanity may be proud of and not ashamed – which looks with suspicion necessarily upon that calling in life and that kind of business, because there is necessarily connected with it more or less deception and deceit."[1]

With Pinkerton and his focus on honest techniques, that attitude changed. His method was based on human nature – the need to tell secrets, to brag, to confess, to ask for help and advise. His agents were chameleons, adept at becoming whatever kind of person the job needed. A lucky gambler, a fellow counterfeiter, a Confederate sympathizer. Detectives must use psychology, a knowledge of human nature. "Criminals must eventually reveal their secrets and a detective must have the necessary experience and judgment of human nature to know the criminal in his weakest moment and force him, through sympathy and confidence, to reveal the secret which devours him."[2]

Pinkerton instructed his detectives in professional skills:

HOW TO SHADOW A SUSPECT SO HE DOESN'T KNOW YOU'RE FOLLOWING HIM
HOW TO DISGUISE YOURSELF AND PLAY A ROLE
HOW TO DRAW OUT SUSPECTS INTO CONVERSATIONS
HOW TO REMEMBER CLUES WITHOUT TAKING NOTES WHICH MIGHT BE FOUND BY THE SUSPECT
HOW TO BE TENACIOUS AND PATIENT AND OBSERVANT, THREE KEY QUALITIES FOR A SPY – I MEAN, DETECTIVE

Kate was particularly adept at playing different roles and Pinkerton assigned her to his most important cases, including thwarting the planned assassination of President-elect Abraham Lincoln on his way to Washington for the inauguration. Kate's role wasn't as pivotal as in the Adams Express case, but having her involved in any way eased Pinkerton's worries.

When Pinkerton was put in charge of the new Secret Service developed under Lincoln to ferret out Confederate spies and to spy themselves on the rebels, Kate was again one of his key agents. Impressed by her skills, Pinkerton hired other women and put Kate in charge of all the female agents and later managing the DC office during the Civil War. Hattie Lawton, who worked under Kate's direction, was sent as a spy to gather information on Confederate army movements, along with Timothy Webster, a top Pinkerton agent. Both Lawton and Webster were caught by the Confederacy and put into prison. Webster was executed as a spy on April 29, 1862, the first Pinkerton agent lost that way. Lawton was more fortunate and was released as part of a prisoner exchange, traded for the notorious Confederate spy, Belle Boyd, on December 13, 1862.

Kate survived her spying missions unscathed, but died young, on January 28, 1868, from pneumonia. Pinkerton was at her bedside. He admired her so much, he had her buried in his own family plot in Chicago. You can find her grave in Graceland Cemetery under the name "Kate Warn."

[1] Marcus Klein, *Easterns, Westerns, and Private Eyes*, Wisconsin Press, 1994

[2] Pinkerton, *General Principles*, a guide for Pinkerton agents

BIBLIOGRAPHY

Cuthbert, Norma B., ed. *Lincoln and the Baltimore Plot 1861: From Pinkerton Records and Related Papers*. San Marino: The Huntington Library, 1949.

Horan, James D. and Swiggett, Howard. *The Pinkerton Story*. New York: G.P. Putnam's Sons, 1981.

Horan, James D. *The Pinkertons: The Detective Dynasty that Made History*. New York: Crown Publishers, Inc., 1967.

Jeffreys-Jones, Rhodri. *Cloak and Dollar: A History of American Secret Intelligence*. New Haven: Yale University Press, 2002.

Kane, Harnett. *Spies for the Blue and Gray*. Garden City: Hanover House, 1954.

Mackay, James. *Allan Pinkerton, the First Private Eye*. New York: John Wiley & Sons, Inc., 1996.

The Magazine of History with Notes and Queries. Extra Number, no.32, Rare Lincolniana, New York: William Abbatt, 1914.

Markle, Donald E. *Spies and Spymasters of the Civil War*. New York: Hippocrene Books, 1994.

Morn, Frank. *The Eye that Never Sleeps: A History of the Pinkerton National Detective Agency*. Bloomington: Indiana University Press, 1982.

Pinkerton, Allan. *The Expressman and the Detective*. New York: Arno Press, 1976, reprint of 1879 ed. published by W. B. Keen, Cooke: Chicago.

Pinkerton, Allan. *History and Evidence of the Passage of Abraham Lincoln from Harrisburg, Pa., to Washington, D.C. on the 22d and 23d of February, 1861*. Pinkerton's National Detective Agency, 1868.

Pinkerton, Allan. *Mississippi Outlaws and the Detectives*. New York: G.W. Carleton & Co., Publishers, 1879.

Pinkerton, Allan. *Thirty Years a Detective: A Thorough and Comprehensive Expose of Criminal Practices of All Grades and Classes*. New York: G.W. Carleton & Co., Publishers, 1884.

Potter, John Mason. *Thirteen Desperate Days*. New York: Ivan Obolensky, Inc., 1964.

Rowan, Richard Wilmer. *The Pinkertons*. Boston: Little, Brown, and Company, 1931.

Stashower, Daniel. *The Hour of Peril*. New York: Minotaur Books, 2013.

Voss, Frederick and Barber, James. *We Never Sleep: The First Fifty Years of the Pinkertons*. Washington: National Portrait Gallery, 1981.

ABOUT THE AUTHORS

MARISSA MOSS

has written more than 70 books for children. Her popular *Amelia's Notebook* series has sold millions of copies and been translated into five languages. Her books have been **ALA** Notables, California Book Award winners, **IRA** Teachers' Choices, and earned many starred reviews. For more information, go to marissamoss.com.

APRIL CHU

began her career as an architect with a degree from the University of California, Berkeley, but decided to return to her true passion of illustrating and storytelling. Her books have received starred reviews from Kirkus, Publishers Weekly, Booklist, and School Library Journal. Her most recent picture book biography, *Ada Byron Lovelace & the Thinking Machine,* was a Cook Prize Honor title and **NSTA** award winner. April lives and works in Oakland., California. Learn more about her at aprilchu.com